Stutter Speech Therapy Techniques

Fluency Shaping

By DAVE MCALLEN & A. N. OKONOBOH

ISBN: 9798649348348

DEDICATION

To all those interested in the stuttering world.

CONTENTS

ACKNOWLEDGMENTS

Thanks all you stutterer and fans who willingly volunteered your experiences when you were struggling with stammer.

INTRODUCTION

THIS book is a very effective tool for the resolution of the problem. Stuttering seems impossible. But facts have it that it has easy correction. We've replicated this, times without number.

A. N. Okonoboh was a stutterer. He had to beat his tights to get out a single jerky word. Now, he is a fluent public speaker. But he stopped stuttering by force. His father didn't like it, so he beat it out his head.

Okonoboh later found the key to turning off stuttering. Simply, that key is CONSCIOUSNESS. And he initially used it on a few friends. And it's true. He replicated it on others, and it doesn't fail.

Dave McAllen and Okonoboh developed a book out of the experience. It's the book you are now reading. This book does not evolve from hunger for money. It's an honest way of reaching out to those still trapped in a vortex from which escaped is very possible. Okonoboh's findings have been replicated with success.

If you explore this book, you will find that it isn't complicated like most books on the subject because it isn't base on intellectual or laboratory theories. It doesn't contain specialist languages of professionals. It's based just on real-life discoveries, that is working for real people.

You will also find the simple secret as a theme that run through the book. If you can keep them in mind, you will solve not only your problem, but those of other stutterers. The theme or key is: CONSCIOUSNESS, BREATH CONTROL, RECONFIGURATION OF THE SPEECH MOTOR THROUGH SLOW SYLLABIC TALK, RATHER THAN THE WORDS OR SENTENCE SCOPE.

DEFINITION

WHAT is stammer? In the context of this course, we would like to define stammer as the inability to coordinate the speech organs to say the first sound. This problem usually results in stopping and attempting to say the word several times before saying it correctly.

However, our study doesn't understand normal stammer to be distortion of the organs of speech themselves. These organs in almost all cases are in good working order. That is why it is no wonder that a stutterer may speak fluently on certain occasions, but dysfluently at others.

CAUSES OF STAMMER: There are five major causes of stammer. They are: Heredity, Lack of confidence and poise, Imitation, Poor foetal muscular development, and Nervous breakdown.

(a) Heredity: A gene for stammer was discovered recently by scientists around 2012. This means that some people stammer because they acquire the trait through the family thread and the gene is not recessive in them. This is a factor in most of the people who stammer.

Stammer acquired by heredity tends to be severe. When spotted early in the child, however, parents or caregivers can help the child before the condition is rooted in the him.

(b) *Lack of Confidence and Poise:* Some people stammer when they face a large audience or someone who in their judgment is formidable. Overtime, if not conquered, such phobia and anxiety can create a new synapse in the brain to recognize them. Thus the brain automatically send responses back to the body through this imprint each time this person faces the frightening situation. This causes him to stammer.

This case of stammer is usually not severe. And the stuttering occurs during only selected occasions. The brain imprint can also be overwritten easily as the sufferer regains confidence.

(c) *Imitation:* Some people also stammer when the closest person to them stammers. In this case, the original stutterer has to be an associate whom they respect, admire and share his values.

This form of stuttering can never become deep-rooted. And the acqirer rarely stutters.

(d) *Poor Foetal Muscular Development:* The muscles play a very big part in our speech. At times some people had problems as a foetus at the stage when their muscles were developing or when the part of the brain that controls the muscles was developing. As a result, they lack the ability to coordinate the muscles of their bodies from birth. By the time they get to the age of speaking, coordinating the muscles that participate in speech also becomes a big challenge.

The case is generally severe. Even with the attention of the best neurologists most of the cases can never be corrected.

(e) Nervous Breakdown: A person who speaks normally can become a stutterer later in life due to ill-health. Most cases are associated with nervous issues. Some examples of ailments that may cause stuttering are Als, Parkinson Disease, Muscular Dystrophy, etc.

When stammer occurs in these cases, the speech condition worsens with the deterioration of the health condition. Because these and similar health conditions can only be managed at present, recovery from stammer associated with them is thus impossible.

BREATH CONTROL

BREATHING plays a very important role in human speech. The speech organs and the participatory muscles in the respiratory system gradually release the air of our breath. The system is so efficient that there is usually no need to breathe in more rapidly to sustain our speech. Except for those who bop to speak because of damage of the pharynx.

We do not say this, however, to oversimplify the task of speaking. A lot of complex activities go on in our bodies unknown to us. Anyway, they are natural and not burdensome.

Yet the quality of speech is sometimes determined by the ability to control our breath, although this control is not a requirement for for a normal speech. But when there is a speech challenge such as in the case of voice training for singers or therapy for those with speech impediments, conscious control of the breath becomes vital in the remedial process. So, stammer, lisping and consonant issues, will normally require breath control knowledge as one of the basic training at the startup level.

This book is focused mainly on stammer and how to correct it, with the exemption of those that originate from the last two causes, namely: Poor foetal muscular development and nervous breakdown.

Learning to control the breath is where the resolution of stuttering starts. As already mentioned, breathing is a major factor in the performance of our speeches. This can be seen in the depth and the clarity of voice. It can be felt in the sound pace, pitch, as well as in the stability of our voice. For example, a shallow breathing causes a clipped or high-pitched sound, while a deep breath produces a thunderous one.

People do not normally worry about the performance of their breath. This is because they speak normally and the mechanisms for their smooth speeches are driven naturally. But if a person stammers, he has good reasons to care. To be able to speak smoothly, a stutterer needs to consciously control his breath until his speech becomes normalized.

Below, this chapter will show just what breath control is about and what should be done to gain the skill.

FILLING THE LUNGS: There are two kinds of breathing. They are: (1) Breathing from the chest and (2) Breathing from the lungs. Either of the two kinds impacts on our speech negatively or positively.

When a person breathes from the chest, he fills only the upper part of the lungs. This affects the amount of air he has in him to speak. This in turn, has a bearing on the quality of the sound he produces when he speaks. Breathing is often this way when a person is anxious or frightened. At this time, the muscles become tensed, including those for speaking. This is what is responsible for a high rate of word jam in a stutterer.

To breath from the lungs on the other hand, requires that the lower part of the lungs be filled first. Then the rising of the rib cage is observed as the filling of the upper part followed. Breathing from the lungs neutralises tension in the muscles. And it is recommended for a stutterer. It also increases confidence and poise.

Having come to understand the kinds of breathings there are, do you know how you breath now? Do you breath from the chest or from the lungs? Try to observe this when you want to speak and you are afraid that the words jam you fear would occur. If you realize it, then, try to be conscious of it each time and try to correct it. Start by sucking in the air to fill the lower part of your lungs. As you continue to suck, you see your ribs expand to fill the upper part. Then, begin to speak slowly and calmly.

Later on, we will dwell in some details on why you need to proceed to speak slowly after filling out your lungs.

VERIFYING YOUR BREATHING: To find out where your breathing originates, place a palm of your hand on the lower part of your belly. It should rise if it's from the lungs and you will feel pressure at the waistline before you observe the rib cage expanding to fill the upper part of your lungs.

Breath control is the primary level of this program. It helps to relax the muscles of the throat, the jaws, the vocal cord and those of the rest of the body. It brings a person to the right mind frame too. Such calmness is groundwork for the muscles around the vocal cord or pharynx to adjust freely. This leads to fewer cases of word jam and less struggle to make the first sound.

Probably you have started learning to breathe properly from the lungs. Why not stand before a mirror sometimes and start talking to your reflection about a subject that often pose some challenge to you? As you do, observe what the mirror tells you about your physical bearing. Does it say that your neck is still rigid? What about your shoulders? Do they droop awkwardly? Your depth of breathing should correct your bearing as you go on.

Another indication of poise and calmness is how the body members are used when you talk. What happens to the hands, the legs, the eyelids, etc? If they are making motions involuntarily and awkwardly, then pay more attention to how you are breathing. Our gestures and facial expressions should communicate meaningfully. If they don't, they draw our listener's attention to us rather than to what we have to say.

Practice! Practice! Practice! Controlling the breath is not going to be automatic. But with practice and conscious efforts, you will gain it and the ability to coordinate your speech organs. And your speech will gradually become smooth.

1. At different time of the day for three months, place a palm of your hand on the lower part of your abdomen for several minutes. Try to observe if you feel pressure from the lower part of your abdomen as

you breathe regularly. Do the same thing cautiously when you are speaking.

2. At different times of the day for three months, practice relaxing the following muscles: (a) Throat muscles, (b) The jaws muscles, and (c) The shoulders muscles. Achieve this by meditating on yourself as you take deep breaths in and out. Do the same thing cautiously when you are speaking.

3. Finally, score yourself for the day.

THE ART OF SPEAKING

STAMMER is not a lack of knowledge of the language structure. The stutterer understands that spoken languages are made up of words. A word may have one or more syllables. And syllables are smaller units of words that produce their own sounds independently. (Examples: Perception = Per-cep-tion and Independently = In-de-pen-dent-ly)

A stammerer's problem is the challenge of assigning a distinct sound to each of these smaller units in his speeches. Therefore, the help he needs is about how to handle syllabic sounds in his speeches.

CHANGING PERCEPTION: A stutterer is often not patient enough to give consideration to the important roles the sounds of syllables play in a speech. Generally, they talk very fast when they have it flowwing and they swallow some sounds when there is an obstacle.

Speaking in this manner, violates the proper use of words units in the speech art. For example. When a person speaks too fast, words are run together which is called slur. The sounds of many syllables are either sacrificed or confused as a consequence. This makes it very likely to hit a bump on the way. Similarly, when some sounds are swallowed, which is often termed muffle, sounds of syllables are also lost in the process. Most of the time, this leads to the self-interruptions that a stutterer experiences.

It is strongly recommended that a stammerer work hard to change his perception and the speed of his speech motor. This way, he would give syllables their proper roles when speaking.

DIFFERING SPEECH SCHEMES: Why does a stutterer's speech becomes rapid or jerky? He has two types of speech blueprints stored in his brain. They are the fluency schedule and the stammer scheme. When he speaks fast, his brain has picked up the fluency schedule. And when he is jerky, the brain is utilizing the stammer scheme. This is a choice that is determined by the environment, his emotional state or his physical strength.

ADJUSTING TO THE RULES: Adjusting actually takes patience and efforts. But the result is clearly seen at every level. It doesn't hide. The more the effort that is put into making progress the clearer the advancement that will be seen.

(a) Learning Patience. Suppress the urge to start talking at once, in a bid to satisfy an audience (an audience can be one person or more) whom you feel want you to say something. This may not be easy because it is what you have been doing all your life. But now that you have a desire to stop stuttering, this is highly recommended.

Learn not to rush yourself for whatever reason. Think

like Narcissus and let your audience wait as for a god as you take your time to give a response. Take a moment to breathe in very deep. This relaxes your muscles, as already discussed in the proceeding chapter. Then start talking, slowly, and continue at a comfortable pace. Never allow others to build themselves up at your expense.

(b) *Counting all the Sounds*. Following the examples given at the opening paragraph of this chapter, mentally break the words of your speech into syllables. Then allow the sound of each of the syllables to come out distinctly in your speech. You might be frightened by the result, a terrible lack of flow. It may even appear that you are learning allover again to speak. Don't worry or feel shamed about that. That is one of the things you are waiting for. It is evidence that you are making progress. In time, you will resume a normal flow of speech. By then, all the words jam that make you stammer will have being eliminated. It is as effective as reinstalling a malfunctioning program on the computer.

Correction of the speaking art is not something automatically picked up by the brain. Persistent effort and regular practice are very vital. Remember that habits don't die swiftly. Reconstruct your speech schemes. Learn patience. Always pause momentarily before you start speaking. If you can count the sounds of a statement no matter how affected your speech becomes at first, your jaws and tongue will adjust to proper movement. And each day, you will see your victory over stammer very near to you.

Exercises

1. Reduce the following words to their syllables and try to say their sounds without stumbling on the way.

Community.

Broadcasting

Comprehensively

Organization.

Idiosyncrasy.

2. Look for opportunity at different times everyday for three months, to converse with someone. Observe how slow and patient you are able to keep yourself each time. Then score yourself with your performance on a scale of hundred.

3. Tell someone to listen while you talk to him. Have him check for evidence of slurring, muffling and the degree of syllabic sound clarity. Then, tell him to score you with your performance over one hundred.

4. Make your own note of words you wish to break down to their component syllables. Prepare your

own worksheet. Practice sounding each syllable distinctly. Graduate from syllables to words, then sentences and paragraph scope. Continue to do this until you are through with this course.

DEALING WITH COMMON OBSTACLES

THIS chapter is designed to help you identify the major obstacles that impede the flow of speech and the practical things to do under each situation. It is in three levels: (1) An extemporaneous discussion, (2) Interruption handling skills and (3) A second extemporaneous discussion. The benefits of recording midgets will also be introduced at this stage. The chapter will conclude with your bearing as a speaker.

AN EXTEMPORANEOUS DISCUSSION: This has to do with talking or handling a speech without reading the subject material from a manuscript. It means speaking, using the words of your normal everyday style in which your word choice comes spontaneously.

(a) Selecting your materials: Select a topic from a book that deals with one of your favourite subjects. Take a day or two to study a selected topic until you are familiar with the main ideas. Next, make a note. The note should not be detailed. It should contain only a few words and phrases that at a glance may help you recall the main ideas in the topic you have studied. You don't need to recall the exact wordings of the author.

(b) *Preparing your material:* Practice your delivery out aloud in front of a mirror using the small note in your hand. Try to apply the skills you already learned at every point to your reflection in the mirror. Take a few deep breaths at the beginning. Observe that the muscles of your shoulders, the neck and the jaws are relaxed enough. Observe your level of patience before you begin to speak. Start slowly and make sure the sound of every syllable comes out precisely. Remember not to care about the lack of flow at this time. Fluency will return later by itself. Take ten to thirty minutes each day to prepare your delivery out aloud, until you are personally moved at heart by the beauty of the content.

(c) *Selecting your audience:* Next, decide whom you will like to discuss your material with. At first, it is usually best to look for a friendly audience. Think of one or two friendly faces among your friends or family and arrange to present your speech to them through extemporaneous delivery style. The audience number might be increased in time as desired. They will also come from any circle later, whether a person of the opposite sex, an older person, your boss or one whose show of knowledge is intimidating. By then you will have gained confidence and poise.

(d) *The speech presentation:* Stand upright before your audience. Take a moment for a few deep breaths. Look at your audience and pick out the most friendly of the faces. Start slowly, speaking to that one first, until you are absorbed into your speech.

How did you do? Compare your achievements with

the past and rate yourself.

INTERRUPTION HANDLING SKILLS: (Have you completed the first assignment on extemporaneous discourse? **Note**: If you have yet to do so, please do not proceed to reading what's in this section. You must identify core problems inhibiting normal speech flow first. Then you will be guided through the process of resolving them here.)

Did you notice something about your final delivery in front of your friend(s)? No doubt, you have recorded marked improvement in your speech. You were more relaxed because your muscles were calmer than you ever experienced. You avoided rushing yourself too, because you tried to be patient and you were speaking slowly. And your words were not slurred and the sounds of syllables were not muffled. This is well commendable.

But you must have observe something which we know. But these things are vague most of the time. So, you might not be able to determine how they sabotage your effort until we put some construction to the matter. They are the major obstacles largely responsible for your jerky speech. They come to play each time you stumble over words. There are three of them. (1) Brake Failure, (2) Regression and (3) Semantic noise

If your stammer condition is the serious type, you no doubt had interruptive word jam several times during your speech delivery assignment above. What did you do? You went back in the sentence struggling to repeat some of what you had already said. This is called regression. Also, you did not pause for a breath. You cracked at the words, instead. This we term "bake failure." In some cases, you improvised some sounds to fill some of the long empty spaces instead of a pause. Some of these sounds were: "emmm," "you know," "so," "uuuuh," "you see," etc. These undesirable sounds are called semantic noise. All three are saboteurs to the efforts to be fluent in our speech.

What then is the practical thing to do whenever you suffer a word jam? How can you avoid brake failure, regression and semantic noise?

(a) How to say "no" to Brake Failure: At once, cut the word that tries to twist in your mouth. Take your time to suck in air deeply. Then start to speak again, at a slow and relaxed pace. No matter how long you paused before you begin, your speech is more beautiful that way.

(b) How to overcome regression: There is no need to go back and repeat some words or phrases that you have already enunciated clearly before you hit the obstacle. When you resume your speech, begin exactly with the last word where the interruption occurred. This makes your speech tidy. As in the case of Brake Failure, it doesn't matter how long you waited before resumption.

(c) Eliminating Semantic Noise: You already know what those noise are. Any undesirable sound that compulsively finds its way into your speech to fill an embarrassing pause gap is a noise □ "emmm," "you

know," "so," "uuuh," "you see," etc. They do not contribute anything to the objective of your speech. They rather distort it and make them awkward. So, no matter how long a pause, it is best to leave the interval blank. You can verify the truthfulness of this matter by making a recording of both situations. You can also listen to interviews and judge for yourself.

Summary note: 1. Cut the words at once, 2. Resume your speech exactly with the last word where the interruption occurred, and 3. It is best to leave the pause interval between expressions blank.

A SECOND EXTEMPORANEOUS DISCUSSION: At this point, take another speech assignment.

Follow the same method as in the first assignment. But select a different topic. Gather your materials for the subject and prepare the contents. Review the rest or the process in the first extemporaneous discussion. Then, during your delivery in front of your audience, (remember that your audience can be one or more persons) show that you have applied practically, the elements just discussed. Strive to make this presentation better than the previous.

Make your comments on:

(a) Brake Failure ....

(b) Your Level of Regression ...., ...,...,. ....

(c) Eliminating Semantic Noise ....

BENEFITS OF RECORDING MIDGETS: Recording and preserving your voice is very important in this course. It is a great way to keep track of your progress. This is not to say that it is impossible to monitor your progress without recordings. No. You can daily see the positive changes in your speech.

Recordings will however give you a more graphic view of these improvements. With it, you can make comparisons with your previous performances. Areas of serious flaws would easily be brought to the fore. And newer recordings will give you much encouragement for which to commend yourself. The more you have something for which to commend yourself, the more strength you will get to go on.

We are fortunate today to be living during a time when recording midgets and devices are there for the taking. Why, even the simplest of mobile phones has an audio recorder built in it. So, getting a device won't be a challenge. Put these to good advantage and record the quickest and best results from the course.

YOUR BEARING AS A SPEAKER: You don't need to be a professional public speaker. But you must talk to people as you go about your daily activities. Whether you are talking to a very familiar person or a personality that's alien to you, your body members play their roles. So, they need to be consciously coordinated when we speak.

It could be very awkward to shuffle the feet and look

at the floor while talking to someone. Don't allow your eyes to bulge out of their sockets because of forcing yourself to satisfy someone who looks on. It is not a good sight also, to stick the tongue out of the mouth in an attempt to say something. Again, how would the person listening to you view you when you slap your thighs or his shoulders to talk to him? Some stammerers shuffle their hands in and out of the pocket.

This can distort your posture. But one or more of these happen often when a stutterer tries to express himself. They are evidence of nervousness and a lack of poise.

Remember though that you want to impart something valuable to your listener. If your bearing is awkward when you speak, the attention of your listener will shift from what you are saying. Instead, it will rest on you. Your listener will begin to sympathize. The experience might not be too pleasant. Sometimes, you may even look stupid and dejected.

That is why you need to care about your bearing when you speak. The only way to solve this problem is to use breath control techniques to relax your body and to be alert to what you do with your body members during your talks.

In a short time, the frequency of your word jams will go down drastically. You need to be persistent and consistent.

Watch yourself. You will find that you won't see those noise again when you speak. Gaps of pauses between statements will close. And you won't make any regressions as you talk. Fluency will soon return to your speech. And you will regain your voice.

HOW OTHERS CAN HELP

FRIEND: IS there someone with whom you spend a considerable amount of time every day? Is the person interested in seeing you succeed in this battle one day? And would he be willing to lend a hand of support? If yes is your answer to all three questions, you are speeding on your way to recovery.

Assign him a role. He can give you a signal to pause each time you are trying to force yourself to continue an obstructed statement. It will be a great complement of your your personal efforts. The prompts will help you take actions when you forget.

THE ROLE OF PARENTS: "One begins to coil the tail of a dog when it is still a puppy," says an Ishan proverb. So, when proofs of stammer are spotted in your little child when he is still tender, get to work at once. Help him from infancy to break the unkindly yoke of stammer.

Researchers have established that the root of most stammer cases goes back to childhood. So, if parents are observant and play their roles early enough in the child's life, cases of stutter today would be reduced drastically.

The child's mind is flexible and is thus malleable. All that needs to be done to help him is the reminder to pause when he cracks at a word and to encouraging him to say it again. He might also be helped to say the last statement. After saying it, he my be asked to say it the way it was said by the tutor. This way, replacing the stammer synapse in the brain, would not be a problem for the child as he grows. The parents that have come to us, all recorded success in this regard.

The message need to reach all parents throughout the globe to to stop making the mistake of leaving the matter of stammer in their child to chance. It should not be hoped that he will give it up as he grows. True, stammer is short-lived in most children even those with the gene. Still, knowing which child will carry it further than the early stage, is as difficult as trying to identify a cock among unhatched eggs.

Parents, do your best early, to forestall problem for your child. The time invested is something you will never regret.

CONSONANT ERRORS

CONSONANT error is the loss of certain consonants or the misreading of one as another in the sound of a word according to the degree of tongue rolling ability. The problem is mostly hereditary.

For a number of reasons, the problem is not an alarming one. In some cases, certain ethnics or languages do not have some consonants because of the language structure. And anybody raised in these languages inherits this loss. So it won't bother many natives except a few who make effort to regain the loss. The Yoruba speaking tribe of Nigeria is a good example. The Yoruba language structure does not have room for the letter "V." So whenever a situation calls for "V" the Yorubas improvise "F."

But for a person who must speak languages other than his native tongue, there are compelling reasons for concern. It is not just enough to speak another language but the way it is spoken matters a lot. Improper enunciation of words can result in broken ideas or even a change of meaning altogether.

Can the word "Glory" retain its distinctive sound if it is pronounced by someone without "L" and "R" sound? What is likely to be sounded is "Goi," which can easily be mistaken for "going."

How can improvement be made? Well, if you know of an Obsessive Compulsive Disorder sufferer what would you recommend for him? Stain himself with what is most repulsive to him. In a similar vein, a person who suffers from consonant errors should pick out the ones that pose challenge to him. After that is done, he should endeavour to play with each, practicing rolling the tongue to get the particular consonant sound the right way.

A person with "R" error can begin with ri-ri-ri... Then, rrrrrrrrr... For a person who lisp, it suffices to be alert when about to pronounce "S" and "Z" and to get more room for the tongue before pronouncing them.

With dedication and practice, a person with these errors can learn to adjust and roll the tongue properly.

Exercises

1. Several times every day, for three months practice rolling your tongue in every way. During this period, try also to sound the letters that give you special challenge.

2. Try to roll your tongue towards the sounds of certain consonants.

3. On the sheet below, list all the consonants that you need to work on.

9 798649 348348